Mommy Yoga

Mommy Yoga

The 50 Stretches of Motherhood

Julie Tilsner

•

Illustrations by
Susan McKenna

CELESTIAL ARTS
Berkeley | Toronto

Celestial Arts
Box 7123
Berkeley, California 94707
www.tenspeed.com

Distributed in Australia by Simon and Schuster Australia, in Canada by Ten Speed Press
Canada, in New Zealand by Southern Publishers Group, in South Africa by Real Books, and
in the United Kingdom and Europe by Airlift Book Company.

Library of Congress Cataloging-in-Publication Data
Tilsner, Julie.
Mommy yoga : the 50 stretches of motherhood / Julie Tilsner ; illustrations by Susan
McKenna.
p. cm.
Summary: "Spoofing on yoga vernacular, presents 50 illustrated poses that capture the
amazing positions mothers find themselves in while feeding, cleaning, and generally caring
for their kids"—Provided by publisher.
ISBN-10: 1-58761-254-2
ISBN-13: 978-1-58761-254-1
1. Child care—Humor. 2. Motherhood—Humor. 3. Yoga—Humor. I. Title.
PN6231.C3T55 2005
818'.602—dc22   2005010501

Printed in China
First printing, 2005

1 2 3 4 5 6 7 8 9 10 — 09 08 07 06 05

For Dawn Wallace—

mommy, yoga teacher, and my personal spiritual guru.

("A blended mocha cures all ills.")

CONTENTS

ACKNOWLEDGMENTS

A handful of people must be thanked for their help:

Namaste to Alička Pistek, Holly Taines White, and Linda Rodgers for helping get *Mommy Yoga* out into the wider world.

Namaste to my teachers: Tim Tilsner, Yolanda Bain, and Andrea Testa.

Special thanks to my kids, Annie and Jack, and to my husband, Luke, for his constant encouragement and tendency to laugh at all my jokes.

Extra special thanks to the many fabulous moms on my moms' list, who offered up Mommy Yoga poses straight from the chaos of their own "practices." Particular thanks go to Amy Charlson, Debi Clough, Julia Bourland, Fern Reiss, and Dr. Katherine Burns.

INTRODUCTION

I started practicing hatha yoga when I was pregnant with my daughter, Annie. As a limber and perpetual worrywart, I was hooked from the first class. But little did I know then that my real yoga practice would begin with my daughter's birth. Now, almost nine years and a second child later, I consider myself a yogi—a master practitioner of the ancient art of Mommy Yoga.

It's been said that kids are natural yoga practitioners. But if you accept that, you must also cop to this basic truth: we are their props. If we sit on the floor, they'll crawl all over us. Sit on a chair, the bed, or the toilet, and it's only a matter of moments before they're on our laps. We're their ladders, their sherpas, their human Kleenex. As I sit here writing this, my four-year-old is standing behind me on the chair with one leg over my shoulder, trying to climb over my head and into my lap.

Mommy Yoga: it's what we do. And it's a practice we maintain daily until our charges hit adolescence and no longer want anything to do with us. Any mom who's tried to answer the phone while nursing the baby and keeping the toddler out of the oven is a Mommy Yoga practitioner. Any mom who's ever carried three small children, a gallon of milk, and a jumbo bag of diapers across a crowded parking lot is a Mommy Yoga enthusiast.

But then if you're holding this book, you get it. You understand the cosmic truth that motherhood, at bottom, is one long, level 3 yoga pose.

HAPPY BABY

Lie in Savasana pose with legs spread. When birth pain miraculously stops, float on astral plane for several minutes. When nurse arrives, slowly open your eyes and gaze upon the face of God, who for some reason looks a lot like a cross between your husband and Aunt Agnes. Realize it's your baby. Experience nirvana until OB starts on the stitches.

MUMMY

Wrap newborn in giant newborn diaper, Onesie, head cap, and three receiving blankets.

Advanced modified pose: Figure out how to strap wrapped infant into huge new car seat.

BAYWATCH

Stand in Mountain pose—feet planted on the ground, arms at your sides—and gaze into a full-length mirror. Look past the state of your belly and bring your focus instead onto your amazing new cleavage. Take a deep breath. Wow.

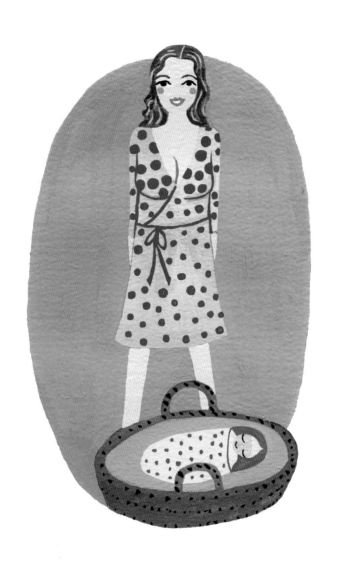

WEEPING WILLOW

Take a deep breath, lower down into Utkatasana pose,
finally falling into a comfy sliding rocker. Hold newborn
in your arms. Cry when your husband leaves for work.
Watch slumbering infant for 2 hours straight. Cry. Listen
to the James Brown CD a work colleague sent over. Cry.
Think about leaving the house to run to the store. Cry.
Repeat throughout first week or two.

WARRIOR ONE

Hold infant in whatever pose works best for you today. When baby latches on, take a sharp inhalation and hold for 30 seconds. Now breathe out slowly. Relax your mouth and jaw. Smile! Float above the pain. Slowly turn your head to regard infant. Focus. Hold for 20 minutes. Repeat on other side. With practice, the pain should subside in 10 days, or whenever the appropriate calluses have formed.

AWAKE

Lie in bed. Listen for baby's cry as partner snores beside you. When you achieve maximum warmth and drowsiness, hear a cry and quickly roll up to sitting. Repeat throughout night.

DUNG BEETLE

Hold your breath. Remove poopy diaper from baby. Wipe baby's bottom using a gentle upward motion and put the used wipes in the diaper. Roll diaper up into a little ball. Deposit into diaper pail. Exhale. Repeat 7 to 10 times daily.

BREATHING EXERCISE #1

In rigid upright position, stare down into bassinet and will newborn to continue breathing using your own breath. Concentrate on the chest area, as movement can be subtle. In. Out. In. Out. Hold pose until further notice.

KANGAROO

Stand with baby in front pouch or sling.

At the first hint of a cry, sway to and fro.

As cry continues, hop up and down.

Repeat as necessary throughout day

and night.

SHERPA

Gather diapers, wipes, blankets, a change of clothes, two hats, three binkies, five burp cloths, an extra bottle of expressed milk, cash, and your keys, cell phone, beeper, and religious good luck medallion to your person in preparation for short outing to the park. Don't forget baby.

TORMENTED WARRIOR

Sit in nurse's chair with baby on your lap, extending her leg outward. Inhale sharply as the nurse approaches with the first of four vaccination shots. Hold your breath and stare at the ceiling as the shots are administered to now-screaming infant. Repeat mantra: "Hurts me more than it hurts you. Hurts me more than it hurts you." Relax your jaw and take care not to bite through your lip.

NAP

Sit in Lotus position and stare numbly at dishes in sink, pile of laundry, and stack of bills. Listen to the pattern of your own breath. At the first sound from awakening infant, slowly come to standing. Repeat twice a day.

GENTLE BREEZE

Calm your mind. Gently lay your hands on slumbering infant in car seat. Undo straps and quickly insert your hands underneath baby. Lift.

Advanced practitioners only: If baby is still sleeping, press him to your chest to muffle outside sounds and wind and walk stealthily toward the house. Warm the crib sheets using only your will. Hunch over the crib and slowly lower baby. Clear your mind! Cover baby with a blanket and slowly back away, silently, like a gentle morning breeze. Best not to breathe.

SLOP

From a standing position, forward bend to floor and make large wiping motions until all lunch is cleaned up. Slowly curl up, one vertebra at a time, until facing baby again. Accept strained peaches on face with serenity. Breathe!

PROOF

On your hands and knees, crawl around the house looking for ways baby can kill herself. Pick up every pin, every penny, from the rug. Plug every outlet. Remove every dead fly from every windowsill. Continue on into the bathroom and note with alarm all the poisons under the sink. Hold pose until the house is childproofed to your satisfaction.

FLY

Crouch with hands over your eyes as Daddy throws laughing baby repeatedly into the air. Remain tense and ready to pounce to the rescue. Repeat mantra: "Don't drop baby. Don't drop baby." Relax your jaw. Concentrate on the lesson that Daddy's way of amusing baby is okay too (probably). Try looking away.

CROCODILE

Hunch over baby on the bed, changing diaper. Dash into the hallway to answer the ringing phone. When baby suddenly turns over by herself, *leap* across the room, arms extended, and land flat on the bed just in time to catch baby as she falls. This is a one-time-only pose. Buy a cordless phone that afternoon.

GOLDEN BRIDGE

Taking a deep breath, stand on tiptoe and dive deep into the crib, holding your stomach muscles away from the rails. Toss all blankets and stuffed animals out of the crib before attempting to remove the tight-fitting sheet from the mattress. Use your nails as claws if necessary! Rise to standing again, take a deep, cleansing breath, and swan dive back in, clutching a fresh sheet. When new sheet is stretched over the mattress, nurse your bruises for 10 minutes. Repeat as necessary.

SHOWER

Place baby in a bouncy seat just outside the shower curtain. Maintaining eye contact and keeping one foot on the bouncy seat at all times, give yourself a quick sponge bath. Change feet when necessary. Repeat as seldom as once a week.

PRIDE

Squatting on the floor, extend your arms out toward standing baby. Grin wildly and chant, "Come on! You can do it!" repeatedly until baby takes her first steps toward you, at which time leap up to standing and go call Grandma and Daddy. Repeat throughout week or until toddler can bring the phone to you.

UP/DOWN

Squat slowly. Take toddler into your arms and slowly rise to standing. Allow toddler to twist almost out of your arms when she spies a bug on the ground. Bend from the waist and put her back down. Hold for 2 breaths or until toddler wants back up again, whichever is soonest. Squat slowly. Take toddler into your arms and slowly rise to standing.... Repeat throughout day.

DOWNWARD FISH

With feet planted firmly on the floor, bend at the
waist and extend your arms into the toilet bowl.
Scoop out all plastic toys. Rinse as needed.

SWINGING MONKEY

At a brisk walk, take one of toddler's hands while your
partner takes the other. On the count of three, lift
toddler into the air between you, allowing her to pull up
her legs and swing. Repeat until your upper arm and
back scream for mercy. Warning: repetition of this pose
is mandatory.

BREATHING EXERCISE #2

Remain impassive as toddler lies screaming on the supermarket floor. As people stare, remember that desire is at the root of all human suffering. Just as you let go of your desire to gag and hog-tie child, so too will he let go of his desire for the bag of Skittles you denied him ten minutes ago. Any minute now. Breathe!

TRIANGLE

Use a partner for this pose. Lie on your back and practice controlled breathing. Allow toddler into bed after a "bad dream." Lie still until toddler angles himself into Triangle pose and falls into a deep sleep, pushing both you and Daddy off the bed and onto the floor. Crawl to the couch.

BOUGH

Sit in Lotus position. Cradle nursing infant in one arm. Extend one leg for toddler to sit on while you read him *Thomas the Tank Engine* for the seventh time. Use Ujjayi breathing to keep baby asleep. Hold pose indefinitely.

REED

Kneel on the hard linoleum floor and forward arch over child in the bathtub. When water is thrown upon you from child's toy bucket, practice deep abdominal breathing, repeating mantra: "No splashing. I mean it." Slowly stand up and wring out your pants. Repeat pose as needed.

MONKEY

Decide to walk to a nearby destination with toddler. Walk 5 minutes, then slowly bend to kneeling and take toddler onto your back. Carry him the remaining half mile. Breathe!

POKEY

Put your left foot in. Put your left foot out.
Put your left foot in and shake it all about.
Do the Hokey Pokey and turn yourself
around. That's what it's all about. Repeat
throughout afternoon or until you start to
scream.

NO GO

Dressed and ready to go to an appointment, hold baby on your hip and thrust one leg out the front door with confidence that, today, you'll be on time. Freeze and hold when baby suddenly throws up all over herself and you. Breathe through your mouth. Regard now-smiling baby and turn, slowly, until you're back inside. Resolve to repeat pose in fresh clothes, or finish up by reaching into your purse for your cell phone.

WALLET

Open first bill from the day care center.
Catch breath. Bug eyes. Fall down. Repeat
every month until kindergarten starts.

UP DOG

Rise every weekday morning at 6 A.M. to begin the day. On Saturdays, Sundays, and all major holidays, rise at 5:30 A.M. at child's insistence. Repeat for 12 years.

MANY-ARMED GODDESS

Stand in the kitchen and take a deep breath. Prepare curly pasta with no sauce for child number one and Dino Nuggets for child number two. Throw lasagna into the microwave for Daddy. Holding each entrée in its appropriate style of dish, with the correct beverage in the correct color of cup, serve everyone at the same time. Repeat 3 times a day.

REFLECTION

Heavily pregnant with third child, push four-year-old on swing while two-year-old hangs from your neck sobbing because you won't take her down the slide. Shift from foot to swollen foot as children throw tantrums at going-home time. Meditate on what you were thinking.

DON'T MAKE ME
STOP THIS CAR

A twisting pose for advanced practitioners only!
At a stoplight, lift your arms overhead and twist up,
around, and down until you're touching the floor
beneath child's car seat. Search by feel for pacifier/
goldfish crackers/Polly Pocket. When you hear a
honk from behind, quickly unravel to sitting position
and drive forward. Repeat as needed.

LEGO LEG-OH!

Hold one foot in the opposite hand. Try to extract a painful Lego block from between your toes. Hop up and down. Breathe. Repeat on the opposite side later the same day.

PHEASANT

Chase down naked three-year-old boy after bath.
Capture and carry him, upside down, back into his
bedroom for dressing (Batman pajamas tonight).
Repeat every night for the entire year.

HORSE/DOWNWARD-
FACING FROG

Start on your hands and knees, eyes looking down.

Lower your body to the floor to allow one child

onto your back for Horse pose. Hold while two

additional children climb on. Let their weight smash

you to the floor with your arms and legs splayed.

Hold for 5 minutes or until spouse comes your

rescue.

FIRST DAY

Lift camcorder to your eye to film first moments of kindergarten. Note that, in all the excitement, child isn't even looking at you. Wipe a tear from your eye. Repeat every year with other children.

SUN SALUTATION
(SERIES A)

Lift report card to the heavens. Forward bend to pick up bumper sticker. Raise your head and straighten your back. Place "Proud Parent of an A Student" on your car bumper.

WARRIOR TWO

Park your minivan and arise slowly from a sitting position. Unstrap one car seat. Place infant on your shoulder. Unstrap second car seat. Help three-year-old out of his seat, accepting all of his artwork in one hand. Close the door. With diaper bag and purse over one arm and a stack of mail in your mouth, walk to the front door. Realize you've locked your keys in the car. Breathe!

TREE

Stand at the bathroom mirror brushing your
teeth. Hold one leg straight out behind you to
prevent toddler from getting into the toilet
again. Ignore her protests, much as a tree
ignores the wind. Hold until you can distract
toddler with something else.

INSECT

Recline on the couch to watch your program.
Two-year-old starts on your lap, ascends to your
shoulders, tries to perch on your head, crawls
down to your lap backward, then inserts herself
under your thighs. Keep your mind clear.
Remain flexible.

MOUSE

Stand before three-year-old daughter. Curtsy. Agree that you are Belle and she is the Little Mermaid and that you are having a tea party for your friends the Little Ponies. Repeat—verbatim—everything she tells you to say, for several months, or until she grows out of the princess stage.

WARRIOR GODDESS

Hunch over a tiny instruction booklet. Find the English translation. Insert prong A into prong F and use the enclosed tool to tighten cogs in slots B, D, and 8C as young boy dances around you asking, "Is it done yet? Is it done yet?" When correctly done, pose results in Kag-Soluth, Battle Warrior of the Fourteenth Dimension Action Figure, which will dominate the world, or at least placate four-year-old until dinner.

FUND-RAISER

Take a deep breath and relax your shoulders.
Hawk Girl Scout cookies for seven-year-old,
chocolate for kindergartner, and Christmas
wrapping paper for preschooler. Repeat every
year until college. Smile!

MOM OF TWO

Stand with your feet slightly apart for balance. Hold nursing infant in one hand while stroking the hair of jealous sibling with the other. Repeat mantra: "Big boys drink from cups." When the phone rings, switch infant to your other breast, holding the phone between your shoulder and cheek, and keeping your hand on jealous sibling's head. Repeat throughout day.

POUCH

Stand before a full-length mirror, inhaling deeply and sucking your large stomach pouch in as far as you can. Tell yourself you love your new body and, really, it's not so bad, is it? Swear under your breath that you'll start Pilates tomorrow. Or maybe Tuesday.

HALF-BRIDGE

Lie on your bed, knees bent, with your feet spaced evenly before you. Taking a deep breath, raise your hips and arch your back, pulling your prepregnancy jeans up as far as they will go. Slowly rise to standing, breathing through the discomfort as well as the sight of the alarming gap between button and hole. Try to inhale. If you cannot, quickly roll jeans off and resume Pouch pose for inspiration.

BLISS

Arrive home after a long day. Pause and take a deep breath at the door. Hear the growing stampede of little feet and the cries of "Mommy's home!" Lower to a crouch and let children slam into you, wrap their arms around your neck, and pull you down onto your knees. Kiss their little faces and nuzzle their soft heads (bath night!). Make yourself comfortable on the floor and take children into your lap so you can hear both their stories at once. Hold pose forever.